MW01181380

Ideas for
Spreading
Love at Lunch

Jane C. Jarrell

Artwork by Lila Rose Kennedy

HARVEST HOUSE PUBLISHERS
EUGENE, OREGON

To Barclay Leggett Brunson

31 Ideas for Spreading Love at Lunch

Text Copyright © 2000 by Jane C. Jarrell
Published by Harvest House Publishers
Eugene, Oregon 97402

ISBN 0-7369-0220-1

Artwork designs are reproduced under license from © Arts Uniq'®, Inc., Cookeville, TN and may not be reproduced without permission. For information regarding art prints featured in this book, please contact:

> **Arts Uniq'**
> **P.O. Box 3085**
> **Cookeville, TN 38502**
> **800-223-5020**

Design and production by Garborg Design Works, Minneapolis, Minnesota

Scripture quotations are taken from The Promise™ copyright © 1995, Thomas Nelson, Inc.; from the Holy Bible, New International Version ®, Copyright © 1973, 1978, 1984 by the International Bible Society. Used by permission of Zondervan Publishing House; and from the New American Standard Bible, © 1960, 1962, 1963, 1968, 1971, 1972, 1973, 1975, 1977 by The Lockman Foundation. Used by permission.

Parents, please note: Some of these lunch ideas include toothpicks to hold lunch items together. Please be sure to use discretion when feeding these lunches to little ones.

Printed in China.

00 01 02 03 04 05 06 07 08 09 /PP/ 10 9 8 7 6 5 4 3 2 1

31 Ideas for Spreading Love at Lunch

This little book is meant to be a gift to parents and children. For parents, it provides well-balanced, creative menu plans that are easy to make and fun to give. For children, it gives a different twist on the ol' brown bag with yummy theme lunches and special "You Are the Best" messages. These little messages are uplifting and age-appropriate affirmation morsels that offer both moral support and love to your children.

Menu items that include the recipe are marked with a heart. All the other recipe items may either be store-bought or made from a good, general cookbook.

All the lunch ideas were designed with your grocery list in

mind! Included are easy-to-follow recipes and inexpensive, quick treats that can be tucked into lunches during meal preparation.

These days, kids have lots of choices, but many parents still prefer the more eco-nomical and often more nutritious "homemade" lunch. You may have no control over the foods your children trade at lunch, but at least you will know that you sent them out the door with a well-balanced and lovingly prepared meal with an *a la carte* "happy for the heart."

Packing Tips

Handy Things to Have on Hand

Brown bags, insulated bags, or lunch box

Single serving plastic containers with airtight lids

Small plastic containers with lids for dressings, dips, and peanut butter

Aluminum foil

Plastic utensils

Colored plastic wrap

Water bottles

Thermos

Refreezable cold pack

Wax paper

Small self-sealing sandwich bags

Planning Prevents Panic Packing

Make a list of lunchtime family favorites. Keep your list close at hand so you can plan items that are special in your home. Try posting the list on the fridge so no unexpected items will be found lurking in the corners of the lunch box.

Make the planning process a family time. When everyone participates in menu planning, the cook receives fewer complaints.

Streamline the chopping process. Vegetables like carrots, celery, and broccoli can be cut up in large quantities and packed in individual portions.

Make sandwiches ahead and freeze them. If the sandwich items could make the bread soggy, package them separately and include plasticware for lunchtime assembly.

Make double batches so you can have enough food for more than one meal. This is also great because it involves only one shopping trip and one cleanup.

Bold and Cold

Try freezing juice boxes to help keep lunches cool, but be sure to check on your child's lunch period to assure a complete thaw.

Make the lunch the evening before to assure that it is thoroughly chilled.

Refreezable ice packs are great, but be sure and place each one you use in a plastic bag first to keep dampness out of the lunch box.

Refrigerate the thermos at least one hour before adding cold items.

Chilled salads can also be placed in the thermos.

The Hot Spot

Before packing hot items into the thermos, preheat it by filling it with boiling water and letting it sit while you are heating the lunch item. Empty the water from the thermos and quickly fill it with the entree. Close the lid tightly.

Let's Play Dress Up

Pineapple Cream Cheese Dress Up

1/2 cup crushed pineapple, drained
8 ounces cream cheese, softened

Combine
  ingredients
    in a small bowl and mix well.
Store Cream Cheese Dress Ups in an
  airtight container in the refrigerator.

8

Fresh Fruit Cream Cheese Dress Up

1/4 cup strawberries, chopped
1/4 cup kiwi, chopped
8 ounces cream cheese, softened

Combine ingredients in a small bowl and mix well.
Store Cream Cheese Dress Ups in an airtight container in the refrigerator.

Herb Mayonnaise Dress Up

1/2 cup mayonnaise
2 1/2 tablespoons thyme or parsley

Combine ingredients in a small bowl and mix well.

Mustard-Honey Mayonnaise Dress Up

1/2 cup mayonnaise
1 tablespoon freshly squeezed lemon juice
1 tablespoon honey
1 tablespoon Dijon mustard

Combine ingredients in a small bowl and mix well.
Store Mayonnaise Dress Ups in an airtight container in the refrigerator.

Pretty Fancy Popcorn

Cheesy Popcorn

2 cups popped popcorn, still warm
2 tablespoons butter or margarine,
    melted
4 tablespoons cheddar cheese,
    shredded
salt to taste

Combine ingredients in a self-
    sealing plastic bag
    and shake to
    combine.

Fruited Popcorn

2 cups popped popcorn
2 tablespoons butter or margarine,
    melted
1/2 cup dried apricots, chopped
1/2 cup golden raisins

Combine ingredients in a self-sealing
plastic bag and shake to combine.

1 Chunky Monkey

Chicken chunks, ham chunks,
   or hot dog chunks
Vegetable chunks with dressing dip
♡ Monkey chow
Chocolate chunk cookies

Monkey Chow

1 cup dried bananas
1/2 cup dried pineapple
1/2 cup dried apricots
1/2 cup raisins

Place ingredients in a large reclosable
plastic bag, seal, and shake.

Happy for the Heart
Place a small "chunky"
block or small toy in the
lunch box with a note
that reads: "A trip to the
toy store is what we'll
do, to buy a new toy or
book for you."

2 Muffin Madness

♡ Ham and cheese muffins
BBQ baked potato chips
Yogurt cup
Dried cranberry mini muffins

Ham and Cheese Muffins

1 box cornbread muffin mix
1/3 cup ham, finely diced
1/3 cup cheddar cheese, shredded

1. Preheat the oven to 350°.
2. Prepare cornbread muffin batter according to package directions.
3. Stir in diced ham and cheese.
4. Line a mini muffin pan with paper liners. Spoon batter into papers, filling each 2/3 full.
5. Bake for 15 minutes or until muffins are golden brown.

Happy for the Heart
Cut out the shape of an ice cream cone, cut out another shape of a scoop of ice cream, and write on the ice cream scoop: "After-school treat will be ice cream for you and me. You are the sweetest."

13

3 Finger Food Fun

♡ Oven-fried chicken fingers with mustard-honey dipping sauce
Bagel chips
Mandarin oranges
Cheesy popcorn
Flavored water

Oven-Fried Chicken Fingers with Mustard-Honey Dipping Sauce

1 1/2 pounds chicken breasts, cut in strips
1/2 cup milk
2 eggs
1 tablespoon lemon juice
2 tablespoons honey
1 1/2 cup bread crumbs
1/2 teaspoon salt
1/4 teaspoon pepper

1. Lay the chicken strips on a piece of wax paper.
2. Place the milk, eggs, lemon juice, and honey in a medium-sized bowl, stir to combine.
3. Dip the chicken pieces into the egg mixture and then into the bread crumbs (add salt and pepper to bread crumbs and mix together before dipping chicken).
4. Place on a cookie sheet and bake at 350° for 25 to 30 minutes. Turn once during baking.

Happy for the Heart
Create a special cheer that emphasizes the best qualities of your child. Write it down on a mega-phone-shaped piece of paper, and offer to teach it to him when he gets home.

4 Triangle Lunch

♡ Mix and match quesadilla, cut into triangle shapes
Tortilla chips
Cantaloupe triangles
Brownie cut into triangle shapes

Mix and Match Quesadilla

4 small tortillas
butter
1/2 cup Monterey Jack cheese, shredded
1/4 cup chopped chicken, chopped ham, and cooked and crumbled hamburger

1. Spread one side of each tortilla with butter, place two tortillas butter-side down in a skillet, and sprinkle with ingredients. Top them with the unbuttered side of the remaining tortillas.

2. Cook for 1 minute on one side and flip over and cook on the other side until cheese is melted and the ingredients are warm. Cut into quarters and pack tortilla triangles in a warmed thermos.

Happy for the Heart

Place a magnet letter P in the lunch box ("P" is for Park). Tie a small note on the letter with a promise to go to the park after school and feed the ducks, swing, or just sit and talk. (If your child is not reading, cut out a picture of a park and place it in the lunch box.)

"I will provide for you and your little ones."
THE BOOK OF GENESIS

5 Drum It Up Lunch

♡ Oven-fried drumsticks
Fat pretzel drumsticks
String cheese drumsticks
Celery sticks
Ding Dong drum

Oven-Fried Drumsticks

6 drumsticks
1 cup buttermilk
1 1/2 cups seasoned stuffing mix

1. Place the drumsticks in a mixing bowl and pour in the buttermilk.
2. Marinate in the refrigerator for several hours.
3. Place the stuffing mix in a reclosable plastic bag. Place the drumsticks in

the bag and shake to thoroughly coat.
4. Arrange the chicken pieces in a single layer in a nonstick baking pan. Bake at 350° for 40 to 45 minutes.

Happy for the Heart
Place a little foil-wrapped chocolate heart in the lunch box with a note that reads: "My heart beats for you."

"Wheels on the Bus" Lunch

♡ Busy day biscuit sandwich filled
  with shaved ham and sweet mustard
Mini Ritz crackers filled with
  peanut butter
Carrot circles
Mini rice cake sandwich with chopped
  fresh fruit center
Oreos

Happy for the Heart
Cut a wheel shape out of
construction paper and draw spokes
around the inside of the circle.
Write the child's best qualities on
the spokes of the wheel.

Busy Day Biscuits

2 cups biscuit mix
1 stick butter, melted
1 cup sour cream

1. Place the biscuit mix in a medium
   bowl, add the melted butter and
   sour cream.
2. Stir thoroughly to combine.
3. Spoon into a muffin tin and bake at
   400° for 10 to 12 minutes.

Split the biscuits in half and prepare
   sandwich.

7 Kabob Job Lunch

Turkey, cheese, and mini muffin kabob
Fruit kabob
Cookie sticks

Slide turkey chunks, cheese
chunks, and mini muffins
onto a blunt-ended
kabob skewer,
alternating as
you go. This is
a one stop
shop lunch
on a stick!

Happy for the Heart

Make a small coupon book using colorful sticky notes. Punch a hole in the top with a hole punch and tie with a ribbon. Include coupons for a trip to the ice cream shop, a new small toy, a date with Mom for dinner, breakfast in bed, and a stay-up-late movie and popcorn night, all to be redeemed throughout the month.

Number Wonder Lunch

♡ Number pasta salad
Date of their birthday cut out of favorite bread
Carrot coins
Cookies with numbers formed on the top
  with mini candy-coated chocolates

Number Pasta Salad

1 box number-shaped macaroni,
  cooked and drained
1/4 cup cheddar cheese, cubed
1/2 cup mixed vegetables
1/2 cup mayonnaise
1 tablespoon sweet pickle relish

In a medium-sized bowl, combine all
  ingredients and stir thoroughly.

Happy for the Heart
Place a small calculator in the lunch box and attach a note that reads: "You can always count on me."

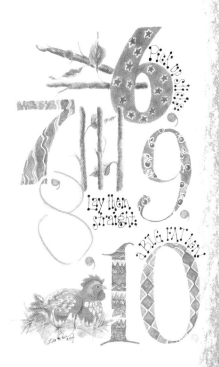

Mexican Munchies

♡ Tortilla roll
Tortilla chips with dipping sauce
Mixed raw vegetable medley
♡ Cinnamon nachos

Tortilla Roll

4 small tortillas
1/2 cup cooked refried beans
1/2 cup shredded chicken
1/4 cup lettuce, shredded
*1/4 cup Monterey Jack cheese,
    shredded*
*Optional: small container of sour
    cream for dipping*

1. Place the tortillas on wax paper.
   Spread the tortilla with the refried
   beans. Top with chicken, lettuce, and
   cheese.
2. Roll the tortilla tightly and wrap with the
   wax paper.

Cinnamon Nachos

Cut two small tortillas into small triangles, butter and sprinkle with cinnamon sugar, and broil in oven until crisp.

Happy for the Heart
Getting a letter in the mail is always a big deal to a child, so what could be better than including a little letter addressed to them in the lunch box? Write a note and place it in an envelope, address it to your child, and draw your own cute stamp in the upper right-hand corner.

10 Bagel Buddies

Mini bagel pizza bites
♡ *Lettuce roll*
Pear slices
Cinnamon raisin bagel chips with whipped honey

Lettuce Roll

1 head romaine lettuce, cleaned and ribs removed
8 slices Muenster cheese
1/2 cup salad dressing
1/2 cup carrots, shredded

1. Lay lettuce leaves on a piece of wax paper.
2. Spread the lettuce leaf with salad dressing and top with the cheese.
3. Sprinkle the lettuce leaf with carrots. Roll the lettuce leaf tightly and secure with a toothpick.

This recipe prepares the whole head of lettuce. You can also add a thin slice of turkey or roast beef to the list to make a main dish lettuce roll.

Happy for the Heart
Cut out the shape of a bagel (don't forget the tiny hole in the center) and write an example of when you caught your child doing something right. Be generous and pour on the praise.

11 Crunch a Bunch Lunch

Chilled taco salad
Carrot and apple sticks
Popcorn and honey roasted peanut mix
♡ *Caramel crunch shortbread*

Caramel Crunch Shortbread

1 stick butter
1 teaspoon vanilla
1/2 cup packed brown sugar
1 cup plus 3 tablespoons flour

1. Melt the butter in a saucepan and brown lightly, remove from heat and stir in vanilla, brown sugar, and flour. Add 1 teaspoon water and mix into a firm, crumbly dough.
2. Place the dough into an 8-inch cake pan and pat into a solid layer. Perforate the top of the dough with a fork.
3. Bake at 375° for 20 minutes. Cool for 15 minutes. Cut into wedges.

Happy for the Heart
Put a thank-you note in
the lunch box. Write a
note telling the child how
thankful you are to have
them as part of your family.

12 Bananarama

Banana bread and cream cheese
  sandwich
Banana chips
Orange wedges
♡ *Banana pop*

Banana Pop

  2 bananas
  1/4 cup peanut butter
  1 cup chocolate chips

1. Cut the bananas in two and insert popsicle sticks in the bottom of each banana half.
2. Spread bananas with peanut butter and roll in chocolate chips. Wrap in wax paper and place in a resealable plastic bag in the freezer until hard.

Happy for the Heart
Help your child develop a "blessings blueprint." Place a card in the lunch box and ask the child to write down 5 things that are blessings in her life. Write your 5 biggest blessings on the other side and be sure to include that wonderful child first.

13 Over the Rainbow

♡ *Rainbow toast sandwich*
Potato chips
Fresh fruit medley
Big piece of chocolate cake with a
* rainbow of sprinkles*

Rainbow Toast Sandwich

   2 pieces white bread
   1/2 cup whipping cream, divided
   Food coloring
   Favorite peanut butter
   Favorite jelly

1. Pour the cream into little containers and add food coloring, then you and your child can paint a rainbow on the bread slices and toast.
2. After you have prepared the rainbow bread, slather on your favorite PB&J.

Happy for the Heart
Place a picture of a rainbow in the lunch box with a little gold foil-covered chocolate coin and attach a note that reads: "You are my pot of gold at the end of the rainbow."

When I send clouds over the earth, and a rainbow appears in the sky,
I will remember my promise to you and to all other living creatures.
THE BOOK OF GENESIS

14 New Zoo Review

♡ Snake biscuits with ham chunks
Monkey chow (see page 11)
Chocolate-dipped animal crackers
Jungle juice (any punch drink)

Snake Biscuits

> 1 container uncooked store-bought
>   breadsticks
> 1/4 cup butter, melted
> 1/4 cup cheddar cheese, shredded

1. Remove the breadsticks from the
   container and place on a cookie
   sheet; curve the dough to resemble a
   snake.

2. Brush with melted butter and sprinkle with cheese.
3. Bake according to package directions.

Happy for the Heart
Using an animal cookie cutter, trace its shape on some colored construction paper, cut it out, and write a note that offers a trip to the zoo.

15 Noah's Ark

Pita boat filled with tuna salad (pack tuna in a separate container to prevent sogginess)

Animal cracker sandwiches (strawberry cream cheese with a small slice of pear)

♡ *Rainbow trail mix*
Rain punch (juice in a box with a label that reads: "Rain Punch")

Rainbow Trail Mix

1 cup Fruit Loops cereal
1/2 cup gummy bears
1/4 cup M&Ms

Place ingredients in a reclosable plastic bag and shake to combine.

Happy for the Heart

Plan a rainbow treasure hunt to begin when your child arrives home from school. Leave his first clue on a red piece of paper in the lunch box. Have four other clues, each on a different color paper, to represent the different colors of the rainbow. At the end of the hunt, have your child's favorite little something.

"Bring into the boat with you a male and female of every kind of animal and bird....Store up enough food for yourself and for them." Noah did everything the LORD told him to do.
THE BOOK OF GENESIS

16 ☼ Roly-Poly

Tortilla and Ham Roll-up

♡ *Tortilla and ham roll-up*
Fruit roll-ups
Blueberries
Malted milk balls

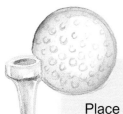

Happy for the Heart

Place a golf ball in the lunch box with a note offering a trip to play putt-putt golf the following weekend.

2 small tortillas
1/8 cup herbed cream cheese
2 slices of ham
2 sweet pickle spears

1. Place the tortillas on a piece of wax paper. Spread the tops of each tortilla with the cream cheese and top with a slice of ham and pickle spear.
2. Roll the tortilla tightly and secure with a toothpick.

17 Deep Blue Sea

Mini submarine sandwich
Dolphin or goldfish crackers
Carrot stick fishing poles
Gummy worms
Roll of Lifesavers

Happy for the Heart
Place a little plastic fish in the lunch box and tie a note on a string and then around the fish. The note reads: "You're such a great catch. How about a trip to the aquarium this weekend?" (If there is no aquarium in your area, go to the pet store and visit the tropical fish.)

What about the ocean so big and wide? It is alive with creatures, large and small....All of these depend on you to provide them with food, and you feed each one with your own hand, until they are full.
THE BOOK OF PSALMS

18 Pasta Pals

♡ *Pasta parfait*
Kiwi circles
Orange segments
♡ *Pasta pudding*

Pasta Parfait

1 package rainbow colored pasta,
*   cooked and drained*
1/2 cup Parmesan cheese, grated
1 cup mixed vegetables
1 jar alfredo sauce
breadsticks

1. Layer one color of cooked pasta in the bottom of a thermos, sprinkle with cheese, vegetables, and alfredo sauce, repeat layers until the thermos is full.
2. Serve with breadsticks.

Pasta Pudding

1 cup thin spaghetti noodles,
*   cooked and drained*
1 cup sugar
8 ounces cream cheese, softened
1 cup butter, softened
8 eggs, beaten
1 tablespoon vanilla
2 tablespoons raisins

1. In a medium bowl mix together noodles, sugar, cream cheese, butter, eggs, and vanilla.

2. Pour pasta mixture into a greased 3-quart baking dish.
3. Sprinkle with raisins.
4. Bake for 1 hour and 15 minutes at 350°.
5. Remove from oven and let cool completely. Cut into squares.

Happy for the Heart
Place some tube pasta and some heavy string in a small plastic bag. Write a note that says: "String the pastas onto the string and tie it on your arm. Every time you look at it remember how much I love you. You're my pasta pal."

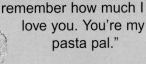

19 Easy As Pie

♡ *Cold cheese and broccoli pie*

*Zucchini circles with a
cream cheese dress up*

(see page 8)

*Peach slices
Cherry pie (store-bought)*

Cold Cheese and Broccoli Pie

3/4 cup cheddar cheese, broken into
small pieces
1 1/2 cups ricotta cheese
1 1/2 cups cottage cheese
1 pound broccoli, cooked and well-
drained

2 eggs
3 ounces cream cheese
1 8 1/2-ounce package corn muffin
mix

1. Preheat oven to 350°.
2. In a medium-sized bowl, mix together
cheddar cheese, ricotta cheese, cottage cheese, broccoli, eggs, and
cream cheese.
3. Place into a greased 9 x 13-inch pan.
Set aside.
4. Prepare the corn muffin mix according
to package directions. Spread evenly
over the top of uncooked pie in pan.
5. Bake for 40 to 45 minutes at 350°.
Remove from oven and let cool.

Happy for the Heart

Cut out the shape of a piece of pie from construction paper. Write a note on the slice of pie: "This pie slice is good for a baking of your very favorite pie this weekend. Remember, anyway you slice it, you're the best."

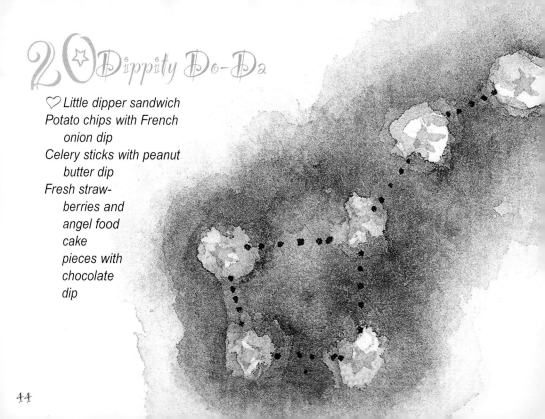

20 Dippity Do-Da

♡ Little dipper sandwich
Potato chips with French
  onion dip
Celery sticks with peanut
  butter dip
Fresh straw-
  berries and
  angel food
  cake
  pieces with
  chocolate
  dip

Wrap the turkey around each breadstick, followed by the cheese and lettuce leaf. Secure with a toothpick and wrap tightly with foil.

Little Dipper Sandwich

2 soft breadsticks
2 slices turkey, thinly sliced
2 slices cheese
2 lettuce leaves
1/4 cup mustard-honey sauce, for dipping

Happy for the Heart
Cut waves in the top of a piece of blue construction paper. Write a note on the "water" inviting the child for a dip in the pool after school.

21 Birthday Bash

Birthday present sandwich (wrap the
  sandwich in wax paper and then in
  birthday paper, tie with a large
  colorful bow)
Heart-shaped cheese
Bag of corn chips
♡ *Candy confetti*
Favorite box of juice

Candy Confetti

1 cup plain chocolate candies
1 cup chocolate-covered peanut
  candies
1 cup white chocolate morsels
1 cup gummy bears
1 cup malted balls

In a large reclosable plastic bag, combine ingredients and shake to combine.

Happy for the Heart
Place two movie passes in a small box, cut out a picture of a new movie that the child is wanting to see. Include a small birthday card that reads: "A special date for a special someone." Ask for a date to dinner and a movie for just the two of you.

22 Mack Attack

♡ Mack truck sandwich
Alphabet macaroni and cheese
Grapes
Gelatin snack cup

Happy for the Heart
This is a "little man's" lunch. Include a match box-sized MACK truck in the lunch box. Cut out the shape of a truck from construction paper. Write on the truck shape: "I'd travel anywhere with you. YOU are the best."

Eat your bread in happiness.
THE BOOK OF ECCLESIASTES

Mack Truck Sandwich

1 large roll
1 slice roast beef
mayonnaise and mustard
4 slices carrots

1. Cut a hole in the center of the roll, remove the center and place on the front of the roll to resemble the cab of the truck. Attach it with a tooth-pick.
2. Spread the mayonnaise and mustard in the center of the truck, fold roast beef slice and place in the middle of the roll.
3. Using toothpicks, stick the carrot rounds around the sides of the roll to resemble wheels.

23 Bow Tie

Bow tie pasta salad (see page 24 for pasta recipe)
Bread bows
♡ *Bacon bows*
Brownies

Bacon Bows

2 slices bacon
String

1. Overlap the 2 pieces of bacon 1-inch end to end.
2. Form the shape of a bow and tie in the center with the string.
3. Microwave the bacon until crisp, cool, and cut string from bacon with kitchen scissors.

Happy for the Heart
On a piece of white paper write: "Look for a special bow surprise when you arrive home from school today." Roll the paper up tightly and secure with a big bow. Tie a large bow around a big tree or around the railing leading up to your porch. Include your child's favorite candy bar in the ribbon.

(For Bread Bows, take breadstick dough from the store and fold into bows before you bake.)

24 Pocket Pals

Ham pocket
Lettuce pocket (salad in a pita)
Kiwi cup
♡ *Perfect dessert pita*

Perfect Dessert Pita

2 pita pockets
1/4 stick butter, melted
1/4 cup sugar
1 teaspoon cinnamon
fresh fruits
mini marshmallows

1. In a small bowl combine the sugar and cinnamon. Brush the pita pocket with butter and sprinkle with cinnamon/sugar mixture.
2. Place on a cookie sheet and toast until lightly browned.
3. Fill cooled dessert pita with fresh fruits and marshmallows.

To prevent sogginess in the lunch box, pack the fruits separately and ask the child to assemble the pita at lunchtime.

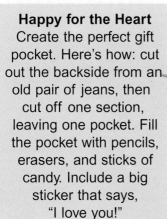

Happy for the Heart
Create the perfect gift pocket. Here's how: cut out the backside from an old pair of jeans, then cut off one section, leaving one pocket. Fill the pocket with pencils, erasers, and sticks of candy. Include a big sticker that says, "I love you!"

25 Fruit to Suit

Fruit kabob with ham rolls
Cinnamon-raisin bagel chips
Apple and pear slices
♡ Chocolate banana bread
    pudding
Lemonade

Chocolate Banana Bread Pudding

1 16-ounce loaf banana bread,
    cut into 1-inch squares.
2 cups chocolate milk
2 3-ounce boxes cook-and-serve
    chocolate pudding

1. Preheat oven to 350°. Place the bread in a 9 x 13-inch casserole dish, pour in 2 cups of the milk, and let stand for 10 minutes.

2. Prepare the pudding according to package directions and pour over the soaked bread. Toss lightly.

3. Bake for 1 hour or until browned and set in the middle.

Happy for the Heart
Cut out a picture of an apple from a magazine, attach a note that reads: "You're the apple of my eye."

The fruit of the Spirit is love, joy, peace, patience, kindness, goodness, faithfulness, gentleness, and self-control.
THE BOOK OF GALATIONS

2.6 Miles of Smiles

Smiley sandwich
Peach smiles
Tortilla grins
♡ Giggles and grins granola

Giggles and Grins Granola

1 cup quick-cooking oats
1/2 cup whole bran cereal
1/2 cup whole wheat flour
1/2 stick margarine
1/2 cup honey
1 teaspoon vanilla extract
1/2 teaspoon almond
   extract
1/2 cup dried pineapple,
   apricots, and raisins

1. Preheat the oven to 300°.
2. Mix oats, cereal, and flour in an ungreased 9 x 13-inch baking dish.
3. Heat the butter and honey until hot and bubbling; stir in vanilla and almond extract.
4. Pour the honey mixture over the cereal mixture and stir thoroughly to combine.
5. Bake until light brown, about 30 minutes.
6. Loosen the granola from the pan with a spatula. Stir in dried fruits.
7. Store in an airtight container.

Happy for the Heart
Decorate the outside of plastic lunch bags with smiley faces and include an extra page of stickers for the child to use at school. Write a little note on an index card or sticky pad that says: "When you see these little smiles remember your family loves you."

55

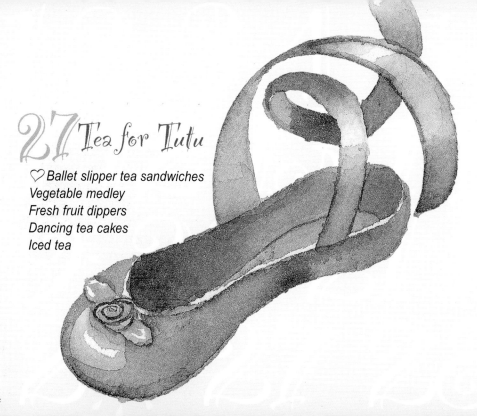

27 Tea for Tutu

♡ *Ballet slipper tea sandwiches*
Vegetable medley
Fresh fruit dippers
Dancing tea cakes
Iced tea

Ballet Slipper Tea Sandwiches

4 slices of banana bread
1/4 cup strawberry cream cheese
1/4 cup strawberries, sliced

1. Slice the banana bread and cut into the shape of ballet slippers.
2. Spread one side of the bread with cream cheese and top with sliced strawberries.
3. Top with the second slice of banana bread.

Happy for the Heart
Gather up a piece of netting into a circle shape (this should resemble a tutu). Tie a note to the little tutu that reads: "You have danced your way into millions of people's hearts."

28 Chop Stix Fix

Egg rolls
Chinese rice (from favorite Chinese restaurant)
Dried apricots
♡ *Chow mein noodle dessert*

Chow Mein Noodle Dessert

> 2 5-ounce cans chow mein noodles
> 1/2 cup mini-marshmallows
> 1 6-ounce package butterscotch morsels
> 1/2 teaspoon vanilla

1. Combine chow mein noodles with marshmallows.
2. Melt the butterscotch morsels in the microwave; stir in vanilla.
3. Pour the melted morsels over the noodles and stir. Spoon large tablespoons full of coated noodles onto wax paper. Let dry.

Happy for the Heart
Purchase some extra fortune cookies at a Chinese restaurant and slide the fortune out of the cookie. (Tweezers are helpful.) Cut a small piece of paper the same size as the original fortune and write an encouraging affirmation on it, then insert it into the fortune cookie for a special surprise.

29 Loaves and Fishes

Mini loaf of wheat bread split and filled with tuna salad
Carrot fishing rods
Fish-shaped pretzel crackers
Gummy worms

Happy for the Heart
Place a package of fish stickers in the lunch box and include a note that reads: "You're a Great Catch."

Taking the five loaves and the two fish and looking up to heaven, he gave thanks and broke the loaves....They all ate and were satisfied.
THE BOOK OF MATTHEW

30 Munch a Brunch Lunch

Egg salad sandwich on a wheat
English muffin
Flavored popcorn
Fresh fruit and yogurt salad
♡ *Raspberry pudding*

Raspberry Pudding

1/2 pound raspberry-filled
coffee cake
1 pint fresh raspberries
1/3 cup raspberry preserves
1 tablespoon butter

1. Preheat the oven to 350°. Slice the coffee cake into 1/2-inch slices and place in the bottom of a 9-inch square pan.
2. Mix the raspberries with the raspberry preserves. Arrange evenly over the surface of the cake. Dot the remaining preserves and butter on top.
3. Bake in the oven for 30 minutes or until bubbly. Serve warm.

Happy for the Heart
Fill a little plastic colored egg with jelly beans. Place a note in the center of the egg that reads: "You're Egg-cellent."

31 Turkey Trot Lunch

♡ Smoked turkey and pumpkin
   muffinwich
Potato chips
Assorted fresh vegetables
♡ Harvest hash

Smoked Turkey and Pumpkin Muffinwich

   4 mini pumpkin muffins
   2 slices smoked turkey
   Favorite "dressed up
      sauce" (see pages 8-9)

Split the pumpkin
muffins in half,
spread a little
sauce on one side of the open muffin.
Top with the turkey and
place the other half of
the muffin on top.
Secure with a
toothpick.

Harvest Hash

1 cup dried cranberries
1/2 cup honey roasted peanuts
1/2 cup mini marshmallows
1/2 cup candy corns

Place the ingredients in a seal-
able plastic bag and shake to
combine.

Happy for the Heart:
Include a Polaroid snapshot
of your child (kids love
pictures of themselves).
Plus, this would evoke a
pleasant memory
from home.

To everyone who is thirsty,

he gives something to drink;

to everyone who is hungry,

he gives good things to eat.

THE BOOK OF PSALMS